Contents

Introduction

Where Did It All Begin?

The Benefits of Meditating

    The Incredible Benefits

4 Styles of Meditation

    Mindfulness Meditation

    Mantra Meditation

    Focused Meditation

    Moving Meditation

How to Start Meditating

    Creating Your Environment

    When to Meditate

    Length of Meditation

    Poses for Meditating

    Final Tips

Ready for Your First Time?

After Meditating

Successful People Who Meditate

A Request...

Other Books by Jenny

Introduction

Meditation is the transformation of the mind.

It is the skill and art of focusing your mind purely on one area.

What do I mean by this?

Well, meditation is the means of altering your mind to promote and develop your ability to concentrate, your mental clarity and your emotional positivity. The practice of meditation allows you to think differently, feel differently and respond to the world around you differently.

Being in a state of meditation is when your mind is completely at peace and devoid of thoughts - whilst still remaining fully aware.

By training your mind to enter a meditative state you are learning how your own mind works and this training allows you to control it. Subsequently this control allows you to do things such as completely empty your mind or focus purely on one thought.

Meditation is a discipline that people often study for a life-time to truly master. This book is not concerned with reaching this level – instead it will cover how you can take the basic principles and practices of meditation and use them to positively change your life.

Practicing even the most basic forms of meditation will have life-changing results and this book will be your guide to get you there.

I wrote this book to distil my years of teaching knowledge into a guide that a complete beginner could pick up, read and understand. The aim for this book is that it becomes the "go-to" resource for people who want to learn the basics of meditation.

I am going to cover everything ranging from the neuroscience of meditation all the way to guiding you through your very first meditation. I also make suggestions and recommendations that I've learned from my years of teaching beginners.

Everything in this book is purposefully written and designed to make meditation as simple as possible. There is literally no one that cannot put into action what I teach and improve their life through meditation.

Where Did It All Begin?

Today meditation is practiced in almost every culture around the world.

Differences in names and processes exist, but the overall concept of positively training and expanding the mind remains the same.

From athletes to the elderly and entrepreneurs to prisoners - people from all walks of life have found meditation to be incredibly beneficial for their body, mind and soul.

But where did it all start?

The exact origins of meditation are hard to pin down but there is evidence to show it comes from the Indus Valley Civilization in India. Archaeologists found wall paintings from 5000 B.C that show people sitting in what we still deem to be the stereotypical meditative pose – the lotus position (crossed legs with hands rested upon their knees).

Although this may or may not be the origin point of meditation, we do know that recently it has spread throughout the world. The concept of meditation has also been adopted by nearly all major religions to aid spiritual development. This is believed to be a driving factor in the widespread popularity of meditation throughout the world.

Moving forward to recent history Swami Vivekananda is attributed to bringing meditation into North America and the popular culture. In the early 20th century meditation saw a huge growth in adoption. This surge combined with growing popularity of yoga (often seen as a sister practice), meant that meditation was here to stay.

And thankfully it did.

The Benefits of Meditating

I wanted to take this chapter to explore the impact that meditation can have in your life and explore the incredible benefits it provides.

Meditation often comes under criticism from people who "don't believe in it" or think it is "spiritual nonsense" that has no backing in science – and thus no place in this world.

I believe these sceptics are born from a deep misunderstanding as to how meditation works and to what meditation actually is.

Once you scientifically study the body and see how it responds to the mind being placed in a meditative state you will see just how powerful meditation can be.

Before I explain the benefits that come with meditation - and how they will better your life - I want to explore what happens to the brain when we meditate.

I think it is important to know this as it will help you better understand why meditation is so important. It also has the use that you can silence the sceptics with scientific evidence – which is always fun!

How the Brain Reacts to Meditation

Let me say up front that I am not a neuroscientist. Also, to try to explain what happens in your brain when you meditate is well beyond the scope of this book. In fact, it probably requires its own book.

However, I can provide you with a brief overview as to what happens in the various sections of your brain when you meditate. This will help you understand why your brains responds so positively to meditation.

Although the practice of meditation has been around for thousands of years scientists have only recently been able to document exactly how the brain responds to meditation.

Using MRI machines researchers have been able to study brains reaction to meditation and everything they've found solidifies what meditators have known (in some vague form) for thousands of years.

So, what happens to the various sections of the brain?

The Frontal Lobe

This is the most evolved part of the human brain and during meditation it switches off. The frontal lobe is pretty much responsible for everything ranging from rationale reasoning and planning all the way to your emotional state.

The Parietal Lobe

The parietal lobe processes and handles sensory information about your environment. As you enter a meditative state the level of activity in the parietal lobe drops rapidly and signal response slows down.

The Thalamus

The best way to think about the thalamus is to consider it as a dam for your senses. It holds back the majority of signals to the brain and lets only some through. As you meditate the thalamus fortifies itself and slows the incoming signals to a drip.

Reticular Formation

The reticular formation handles incoming stimulus and deals with the stimulants as they arrive. It acts as a guard to stimuli and readies the brain against them. By meditating you are lowering the arousal signals and alertness of the brain.

So now you know how each part of the brain responds to meditation you may be wondering how this impacts and benefits you. Well, as the brain undergoes the above changes you will reap the following benefits.

The Incredible Benefits

- Improves Your Focus

- Lowers and Reduces Anxiety

- Increases Your Creative Ability

- Improves Your Short and Long Term Memory

- Increases Your Productivity

- Lowers Stress Levels and Hormones

- Increases Your Feelings of Compassion

- Increases Your Level of Happiness

- Ability to Control Your Anger Better

- Improves Your Mental Clarity and Intuition

- Boosts Your Immune Systems

- Increases Your Energy Levels

The above benefits will change your life and it is no exaggeration for me to say that.

Not only do these benefits have an incredible impact on your health, they also improve your wealth, mental state and relationships.

Meditation is the ultimate brain and life hack.

As you continually enter a meditative state you are actually changing how your brain functions. Not only do you enter a calm state that is amazing for unwinding or de-stressing during the day, but you also promote your body to function on a more advanced level at all times. Something as simple as lowering your anxiety or increasing your creativity doesn't just last for the time that you are meditating – instead it flows into all areas of your life, at all times.

To me the benefits of meditation make it one of the most powerful things you can do to rapidly improve all areas of your life.

4 Styles of Meditation

Now you know all about meditation it is time to explore the various styles.

There are a huge number of different meditation styles that you can adopt. Although they are all focused around the same basic concepts, each style has a few fundamental differences.

In this chapter I will explore four styles of meditation, explain their principles and highlight the main benefits they offer. I chose these four as I believe them to be the foundations on which all other meditation styles are built.

Yes, others kinds of meditation do exist but I feel the vast majority of other styles have their routes in these four. By being aware of these styles you will be well prepared for any future style you come across.

The purpose of this section is so that you can choose which style of meditation is right for you. Choosing the right style of meditation may take some experimentation, but its importance cannot be understated…

Finding the right style for you will deliver accelerated results. It will also mean you enjoy meditation and as a result are more likely to stick to the practice.

I will briefly explain the meditation styles before moving onto my recommendation for which style beginners should adopt. I will then guide you through the process of how to get started.

So, what are the various types of meditation?

Mindfulness Meditation

Mindfulness is probably the most well-known and present form of meditation in the western world. The principle behind mindfulness meditation is revealed in the name – it is all about being "mindful" or aware of the environment surrounding you.

It is a flow style of meditation as you allow your mind to move wherever it wants. In mindfulness meditation you do not attempt to suppress or remove thoughts – instead you acknowledge thoughts and let them drift away. Instead of attempting to block out environmental sounds, such as an A/C unit, you acknowledge the noise and let your mind be aware of it. Doing this will eventually lead to your mind emptying.

While many style of meditation call for you to monitor your breathing patterns, to inhale and exhale in a particular way, mindful meditation does not focus on the breathing itself. Rather it encourages the meditator to be aware of the breathing process, acknowledge it, and continue on.

Mindfulness meditation can be practiced anywhere, standing, seated or lying. Just close your eyes and let your mind drift. After a while your mind will begin to empty and thoughts will stop occurring – some people are aware of this, others are not and liken it to the feeling of falling asleep.

Main Benefits of Mindfulness Meditation

- Creative thinking

- Reduces stress levels

- Increase in energy levels

Mantra Meditation

Mantra is a form of meditation that has the practiser chant a mantra or word during the meditation.

The process of chanting a word or noise provides a focal point that helps the meditator remove external distractions and move into the meditative state

Mantra meditation is different from mindfulness as you are purposefully focusing on one noise in order to remove all other distractions. Doing this empties the mind and allows you to rise above all that is temporary and present.

Making noise may seem counterintuitive to the meditative process; however, remember that the principle is to use noise to create a focal point that blocks out distractions such as thoughts and the environment.

Mantra meditation is best done sitting in the lotus or half-lotus position as it allows for better enunciation of mantras. If you are interested in mantra meditation I would suggest using the "Om" sound. This "Om" sound is the most popular mantra used as it provides a deep vibration within the body that is easy to focus upon.

Main Benefits of Mantra Meditation

- Improvement in focus

- Emptying your mind

- Reducing stress

- Lowering anxiety levels

Focused Meditation

I often think focused meditation is the style easiest for beginners. With focused meditation you place your focus on one singular environmental sound. The environmental sounds can either be naturally occurring - e.g. an A/C unit, or artificially created - e.g. an mp3 of grey noise.

The act of focusing on one singular environmental sound is incredibly freeing.

In our day-to-day life our minds are in 100 places at once, this creates stress and saps both our mental and physical energy. By focusing purely on one noise you hone the mind's focus down and exclude all other thoughts. Doing this will leave you feeling rejuvenated for hours afterwards.

The best way to practice focused meditation is to use an app or track to create ambient noise. Play the sound at a low volume, close your eyes and allow your mind to focus in on it.

Main Benefits of Focused Meditation

- Improvement to focus

- Reduces stress

- Increases energy levels

Moving Meditation

This style of meditation is very trance-inducing. The main difference between this meditation and others is that it encourages movement rather than limiting it.

In most meditations the only movement is the gentle rise and fall of the chest. During moving meditation the focus is on one flowing movement being repeated.

Moving meditation is difficult but it can be very rewarding and energizing. The easiest movement I find for beginners is a simple circulation motion. From a sitting lotus position, allow your upper body to move through a slow circle.

Do not focus on your breathing or your thoughts, instead focus on keeping your body going through the predefined motion.

Main Benefits

- Increased focus

How to Start Meditating

In the previous chapter I mentioned what I deem to be the four main styles of meditation. There exist other styles but those four form the foundations for all other meditative practices.

Now that you know the styles and benefits of meditation you are probably ready to get started.

Remember, this is a beginner's guide, so this chapter will present everything you need to know on how to get off to a flying start in meditation.

Firstly, we have to pick a style of meditation.

I strongly suggest you follow my recommendation and go for a blend of mindfulness and focused meditation. This blend uses ambient noise (focused meditation) and the act of being aware of your thoughts (mindfulness meditation).

If you want to try another style feel free, but for beginners I always recommend this blend. You may choose another style, but, based on my teaching experience, I always recommend this blend of two styles. This style has proven to have the quickest adoption rate, is relatively easy to get started with and produces nearly instantaneous results. Additionally, I believe this style delivers the bang-for-your-buck in benefits.

Whilst I will walk you through every step of "how to start meditating" I will be focusing on my recommended blend, however these instructions will also work for learning all other styles.

Okay, let's get ready to start meditating.

Creating Your Environment

In my opinion and experience one of the most important aspects of successfully meditating is the environment you place yourself in.

Experienced meditators will be able to meditate anywhere – no matter the location. Beginners however will find it very difficult to enter a meditative state unless they make an effort to create and inhabit the correct environment.

Firstly you want to find a quiet place. Some background noise is okay (and can help) but attempting to meditate in your office or busy home will lead to failure. During the early stages of meditation your mind will have difficulty focusing if your environment is too distracting.

I'm making an assumption here that you will be wanting to meditate from your home so I am going to focus on that. If you are going to a class for meditation then your instructor will set up an excellent environment and you don't need to worry about this section.

When choosing where to meditate in your home I suggest that you find a room that you won't be interrupted in. Ideally you also want to draw the blinds so that the sun isn't shining straight onto you.

As I mentioned previously you will be using ambient noise to help you get started and this plays a crucial role in your environment. If you're not sure what I mean by ambient noise it is simply background noise.

There are many apps, YouTube songs and pieces of music you can buy online that will provide ambient noise – I suggest using mobile phone apps as they tend to have multiple tracks to choose from. Pick a noise that suits you (I love the sound of falling rain) and play it at a low level when meditating.

When to Meditate

Finding the correct time for your meditation also plays an important role.

Set an amount of time aside that you are willing to give to meditation each day. When beginning 3 minutes is a good starting point.

You will need to set a specific time for your meditation ritual. I suggest avoiding the "I will practice when I have time today" plan. Usually you will end up missing it as something else pops up and gets in the way.

I find the 3 best times are as follows: morning, noon and night. The benefits of each are as follows.

Morning: It is an awesome way to start the day, it can keep you calm and energized throughout the day. It also gives you the time to meditate on the day ahead and what you are going to be doing.

Noon: This can be an excellent time if you are looking to offload the stress of the day and unwind. Often times we get stressed from all the madness of a busy morning and sinking into a meditative state is an incredible way to relax.

Night: A powerful way to unwind after a busy day. Offload the stress and pressures of the day and use it to escape "work" mode and enter "relaxation" mode. This will help you sleep better and improve your work/pleasure balance.

Personally I like to meditate once in the afternoon for 30 minutes and then again around 7pm just before I begin to unwind and relax for the night.

Length of Meditation

In the previous section I mentioned that a good length of meditation time for beginners is 3 minutes.

This is purposefully short and the reason I suggest it is to form a habit. You may find it very difficult to sit still for 10/15 minutes with no distractions… I mean when was the last time you did nothing, with no distractions and no-one around? This means you are unlikely to continually practice if you dive in at the deep end.

But 3 minutes? That is easy and requires no real commitment from you. I'm sure you could find 3 minutes per day.

This is the key to habit forming - small time investments over a period of five days. If you can do 3 minutes per day for five days you will be well on your way to forming a habit that is hard to break.

After 3 minutes per day for 5 days I suggested the following schedule.

- Increase to 5 minutes per day (ideally twice per day) for 2 days.

- Increase to 10 minutes once per day for 7 days.

- Increase to 10 minutes twice per day for 7 days.

- Increase to 15 minutes twice per day for 7 days.

This process of incremental increases is purposefully done over 28 days as scientific studies have shown that 28 days is the time it takes for a habit to fully grip you. It has been shown that tasks done daily over 28 days will lead to an incredibly powerful habit being formed. Combine this with the amazing benefits you will have reaped and you will find it very difficult to give up meditation.

If you feel you want to progress faster than what I recommend that is fine and feel free to dive into that. One thing I would say is… watch out that you don't drift asleep when meditating. This is something that often happens to beginners when they attempt to meditate for too long too early in their education.

Poses for Meditating

If you were to ask anyone the correct position for meditation they would describe the lotus position. Popular culture and the media has portrayed this as the meditation pose – anywhere you see a portrayal of someone meditating you can almost guarantee it will be in the lotus position.

When beginning meditation people often complain that they can't sit in the lotus position and therefore they can't meditate.

Luckily, sitting in the lotus position is not required and in this section I will cover the other positions that are more suited to beginners. I do suggest that you aim to progress to sitting in the lotus, but don't worry about this yet. Cross that bridge when you come to it.

The first time you meditate I suggest lying down on the floor. This removes distractions, such as uncomfortable positioning and allows you to focus purely on being still.

After a few days of this I recommend moving to sitting with your legs straight out and your back against the wall. This will acclimatize your body to the idea of meditating upright but does not require your upper body to support itself.

Once you feel ready you can progress to sitting with no support and your legs crossed – much like how a child would sit. Initially you will find it easier and more comfortable if you raise your bottom from the ground with a pillow.

Ideally you are working towards being able to sit in the half lotus or full lotus position. Don't rush to this though as you can damage your knees by forcing them into the position before they are ready.

On the next page I have included an image of the lotus position for those who may be unfamiliar with it.

In general the pose you strike when meditating is not important, find what works best for you. As long as you enter a meditative state you will reap the benefits of meditating – sitting or standing.

The Lotus

Final Tips

Now you are ready to start meditating, I want to give you a few tips to follow.

1. Don't expect to feel the incredible benefits straight away. It may take you several sessions before you start to reap all the benefits. This is often a huge stumbling block for people as they go in with high expectations for their first session.

2. During your first few meditations you may not be able to stop your mind racing. This is to be expected as you have been programmed through life to always be "switched on". The best thing you can do is let thoughts enter your mind and sit there. Do not start an internal conversation with yourself – just let the thought sit in your mind, it will drift away on its own.

3. Meditation is tough in the beginning - It is a discipline and as such takes discipline. If you ever think about giving up go back and read the benefits section and remind yourself that good things take time.

4. When you are starting out meditating I suggest practicing in the afternoon or early evening. Beginners often find they will fall asleep if they attempt to meditate too early in the morning.

Ready for Your First Time?

Now that you've read through this book and have a solid understanding on the fundamental principles of meditation, it's time to meditate.

I've explained to you the style of meditation I recommend for all beginners as well as where to meditate and for what length of time. So now it's simply a case of bringing that all together.

First things first, go to the room that you've chosen as your meditation environment and set up the ambient noise. Choose a track that is 3-5 minutes in length.

Lie down on the floor and either lay your hands by your side or interlocked on your chest.

Close your eyes and focus on the ambient noise. Do not analyse the noise, just direct your attention toward it and listen. The natural repetition of the sound will help you greatly.

Breathe naturally or however feels comfortable, don't focus on the inhalation and exhalation, just breathe.

As you do this random thoughts will drift into your head, try not to "think" about these. What I mean by this I mean try not to explore the thought more, just let it sit in your mind, eventually it will dissolve. This is an incredibly hard thing to describe through writing and you probably won't fully understand what I mean until your first time meditating.

Just stay this position for the length of the track. As it ends slowly open your eyes and come back to.

As it is your first time you may not feel anything, in fact you may feel as if you just lay there with your mind racing for 3 minutes. Don't be discouraged by this – it is completely natural and expected. It takes some people longer than others, but by your 3rd or 4th day of this I guarantee you will see huge improvements.

Next up is to follow the rough progression schedule I laid out for you in the previous chapter.

After Meditating

When I finish my daily meditations I love to do a quick two minute stretching routine.

For years I have been teaching and practicing yoga (I even have a best-selling book on it) so my love of yogic stretches is unsurprising. In addition to practicing yoga daily I always stretch after meditating. I feel it helps to further energize me and I suggest you do the same.

I recommend that you follow the brief stretching routine I have laid out for you below.

Hold each pose for 20 seconds before gently and fluidly moving into the next pose. In the following pages I have included images of each pose. This will take you no longer than 2 minutes to complete but the benefits will last all day.

The routine uses very simple yoga poses and is as follows:

- Resting Hands

- Proud Cow

- Morning Puppy

- Sphinx

- The Cobra

- The Mountain

Resting Hands

Proud Cow

Morning Puppy

The Sphinx

The Cobra

The Mountain

Successful People Who Meditate

I wanted to close this book with something I find very eye-opening.

Many of the most successful people in the world meditate. Not only successful people, but world famous successful people.

Given the benefits of meditation it is not surprising that many of the world's most successful people meditate. In this section I've put together a small list (I could have added hundreds more) of highly famous people who not only meditate but also preach how powerful it is and how it's helped them.

People in this list range from musicians to athletes and from politicians to business gurus. As you read through this list you will hopefully have the eye-opening experience I did.

Famous & Successful People Who Meditate

- Al Gore

- Oprah

- Dr. Oz

- Steve Jobs

- Russell Brand

- Sir Paul McCartney

- Hugh Jackman

- Russell Simmons

- Arianna Huffington

- Tim Ferriss

- Ray Dalio

- Marc Benioff
- Andrew Cherng
- Angelia Jolie
- Richard Gere
- Tiger Woods
- Arnold Schwarzenegger
- Hilary Clinton

A Request...

If you've enjoyed this beginner's guide to meditation would you mind leaving me a quick review?

Reviews are the lifeblood of an author's work and even a short one sentence 4 or 5 star review would be a huge help to me. It will only take 2 minutes of your time.

I really appreciate you doing this. I find it hard to express my thanks to people when they leave me a review – but thank you so much.

Kindly,

Jenny Chase

Other Books by Jenny

Yoga for Beginners: A Quick Start Yoga Guide to Burn Fat, Strengthen Your Mind and Find Inner Peace

"Yoga has become increasing popular in recent years - it has been adopted by everyone ranging from children to celebrities and from the elderly to high level athletes.

This wide-spread adoption and love for yoga is not surprising once you begin to understand how powerful yoga can be for both the body and the mind.

What are some of the incredible benefits of practicing yoga?

- Burn Body Fat
- Strengthen Your Muscles
- Tone Your Stomach
- Find Inner Peace and Reduce Stress
- Improve Your Cognitive Functioning
- And Many, Many More

This book is a bible for all things yoga."

All rights Reserved. No part of this publication or the information in it may be quoted from or reproduced in any form by means such as printing, scanning, photocopying or otherwise without prior written permission of the copyright holder.

Disclaimer and Terms of Use: Effort has been made to ensure that the information in this book is accurate and complete, however, the author and the publisher do not warrant the accuracy of the information, text and graphics contained within the book due to the rapidly changing nature of science, research, known and unknown facts and internet. The Author and the publisher do not hold any responsibility for errors, omissions or contrary interpretation of the subject matter herein. This book is presented solely for motivational and informational purposes only.

Images of Yoga Poses: Creative Commons "The Holistic Care Yoga Wiki" by Holistic Care. Used in book in line with Creative Commons rules. File downloaded from Flickr Images edited by Author and Good Living Publishing.

Printed in Great Britain
by Amazon